Satan Sleeps With the Holy
Word Paintings

Satan Sleeps With the Holy
Word Paintings

Carolyn Mary Kleefeld

Introduction,
Collaboration in Editing and Organization
by Patricia Karahan

Foreword by Carl A. Faber, Ph.D.

THE HORSE AND BIRD PRESS   LOS ANGELES

Book Design: Patricia Karahan
Cover Design: Bonnie Mettler, Peace Press
Cover Photograph of the Author: Patricia Karahan
Typeface: Garamond
Typesetting: Freedmen's Organization

Also by Carolyn Mary Kleefeld:
Climates of the Mind
Published by The Horse and Bird Press

Hardbound Limited Edition, signed and numbered	1979
Softbound	
1st Printing	1979
2nd Printing	1980
3rd Printing	1981

Copyright © 1982, by Carolyn Mary Kleefeld. All rights reserved. No part of this publication may be reproduced, stored in a retrieval system, or transmitted, in any form or by any means, electronic, mechanical, photocopying, recording, or otherwise, without the prior written consent of the Author.

Published by The Horse and Bird Press
Post Office Box 67C89, Los Angeles, California 90067

Printed September, 1982

Library of Congress Card Catalogue Number: 82-80785
ISBN Hardbound: 0-9602214-9-2
    Softbound: 0-9602214-8-4

Printed in the United States of America

Satan Sleeps With the Holy
is dedicated to
Patricia Karahan
whose mantic spirit
communes with, answers
the midnight voices of these works

Contents

Foreword by Carl A. Faber, Ph.D. — ix
Introduction by Patricia Karahan — xi
Epigraph by Carolyn Mary Kleefeld — xiii

Prevails a microcosmic soul	1
Alien in whose sensibilities, vision supremely transcend	3
Terror's slave is a tyrant, or, A portrait of the perennial Hitler	5
Whose dignity has been poison-bitten	7
The granite unsupported, falls; boulder-headed	9
From life's otherwise flood of domination	11
Dare Truth's primal drum to beat again	13
The alchemy of transformation is a miracle akin to birth	15
The heavens' blood is sacramental	17
A woo-ing of the soil's constellation's heart	19
Breathes of the pure innocence of the exquisite	21
A holiness doth cling	23
Earnest heirs of star-tipped limb	25
Dies blushing in her lover's red	27
Pulses of white heat's loins	29
The drum of pollination beats	31
I could die with you	35
Never have I known a kiss	37
That unknown design	39
And if you can not, all else is less than What Is	41
You were the summer, long before the Summer came	43
In fevered light	45
Owned by Gray	47
In rest without pause	49
Rhythms of the air's sea	51
But, within me is all of the sea	53
For those who possess their own theater within	55
Our midnight silence fathoms more	57
A broken tree trunk lies next to you in bed	59
Is it here because the malignancy of the benign is contagious?	61
Weapons of well-known strangers	63
Severed from their source	65

Cowards can't resist hate's cheesecloth	67
Stagnates in the swamps of Estrangement	69
At an elegant Swiss Hotel	71
Entrapped; City Lights	73
The Why of the energy shortage	75
The dry rot sucks the forest bare and stays as dry	77
Living my mother's Christ, or . . . Ancestry	79
He betrayed himself	81
The predatory One	83
A marrowless bone, stone of a person	85
The whorling roots of ancestry	87
A testimony to ageless sprout	91
The sea's night does not seem doomed	93
A lone heathen boulder	95
This luminous vessel	97
As is above is so below	99
Nature contains totality's mobile voice	101
Of verdant poets whisper	103
An untamed stillness speaks	105
Accents Nature's integral kinship	107
When Spirit led man's days and nights	109

Foreword

In her new work, Carolyn Kleefeld expresses a celebration and deepening articulation of the sources of Spirit and Transformation. These sources, often spoken of, are seldom understood or illumined. Her poetic vision, however, joins Jung's theoretical formulations to give an enhanced sense of the life and dynamics of Spirit. Welling up in her work is the poetess moved and carried by Nature in all its forms. Again, the integration of Person and Nature receives rare illumination. Some of the phrases are as perfect as the Platonic Forms they describe.

And, we experience again the acute description of beauty and vulnerability in its eternal struggle with Evil, Unconsciousness, and Passivity. The poetic form itself, often soaring in style, gives hope for the individual in this mortal contest. The poetic sketches of character are searing and unforgettable. Truth and beauty have the enigmatic ability to draw the worst of people and the worst from people. These classic battles of Good and Evil, Life and Death, draw sense from her hand.

In the best spirit of wisdom, no simple answers are given. Rather, this poetess provides clear understanding and incitement to the highest battles of integrity and growth.

Bravo Carolyn!

Carl A. Faber, Ph.D.
Venice, California
May, 1982

Introduction

It is rare that one enters the kingdom of God within one's mortal lifetime: an affirmation that such a kingdom indeed exists within one's self. Rare, too, is the creative communication of such singular ecstasy, such totality of Being to others; particularly when those others can then sense that feeling of God within themselves. In her new book, Carolyn Kleefeld lives and conveys both rarities. In so doing, she provides an invaluable gift: a proclamation of the power of the human soul.

Is such a kingdom pure though? Or, in reaching such a height is it inherent that conflict exists, that at the pinnacle of Truth, Evil also has its day. Can one even ascend so high without having faced and confronted within their Self and in the world the primordial power of Evil, of Tyranny, Oppression. And, what is the power, the life force which propels one . . . is it Love, Truth, Integrity, Courage, raw Passion, Intellect, a sense of Death, of Destiny? Can we perceive such forces outside of human beings . . . and be inspired, as in Nature? What becomes of the human in such a struggle; or, what becomes of humans who do not engage in struggle, in conflict, in the Battle with the massive contradictions which are Life.

In this her second book, this numinous poet probes such universal concerns. She does so as a true artist: a person who within herself possesses and dares to live and to communicate the deep mysteries and eternal conflicts inherent in existence.

In her first book, *Climates of the Mind*, she expressed with courage and vulnerability the mysterious process of evolvement, transformation. In this second book, she draws on, dares, and celebrates all the powers arising through such transformation and becomes, in a sense, a force through which primordial, archetypal experience can be expressed. In so doing, this poet symbolizes and communicates the eternal struggle of the living Spirit against forces of Death, and affirms the power and the resulting potential for spiritual triumph inherent in the Individual.

She metabolizes Nature, its quintessential Truth. Through her use of symbolism and allegorical imagery, she communicates the purity and raw power of such Truth, and thus inspires others to sense and to aspire to such an integrated force of being within themselves. She contrasts the alchemy, harmony, natural evolution, and integration of Nature with the discordance which has occurred in humans, and appeals innately to individuals to surmount the human distortions which pose such a ubiquitous threat to Life.

In use of language, and in belief, to this poet, "God" represents a force, a source of infinite birth, which she sees manifested in Nature and inherent in individuals. "Humans" and other words which naturally encompass both men and women are used whenever possible. In some poems, "man" is used instead to maintain a particular rhythm. "Man" in that context also encompasses all humans.

And so . . . in living, as communicated in this book, this poet has merged with the Ultimate, the Divine, particularly in Nature, and too, has tasted, digested, the violence of Satan, of Evil. She does all of this from a place of deep truth, and so emerges as do those rare few, as a keeper and a communicator of the God-fires. Other brave and noble souls may so be inspired.

Patricia Karahan
Venice, California
May, 1982

The singular contains within it, the totality
In experiencing the singular, the totality,
One can experience a serenity only found in the absolute
All of the universe is in one tree, one bird, one flower,
one person

Satan Sleeps With the Holy
Word Paintings

Prevails a microcosmic soul

In the heavens' wilderness primordial
High beyond miasmic grasp
Where barely a human's thumbprint tracks
Prevails a microcosmic soul
Imbuing magnitude unbounded
Breathing primal symphonies of
Orphic breeze and Zephyr's wind
Feathering the winged seed

O genesis of life
Beyond man's demise
You are an aliment for fervent spirits; other Deities,
Impassioned of the blazing eye
Re-creating life as the heavens live

O eternal Renaissance of reincarnations
You scintillate infinite transformations
Veining matter into rhythm's marrow of form

O microcosmic soul; Domed countenance
Within your illimitable cathedral
Of sovereign being, You answer not
For drought or storms
Nor lightning's charring cleave

O spirit translucent
Who bodes in the wake of torch's day
Your face exudes primordial temperaments
Effusing your boundless cathedral
Complexioning archetype and myth
In artless design

O conveyor of evanescent perfection
You are eternal in
Your sublime shadow of expression

Alien in whose sensibilities, vision supremely transcend

In the radical embracing of life
In the assimilation of its marrow with one's own
In blood fusing with experience
In the sublime unfurling of arcana—
In this defining, refining; Transcendence
Simultaneously one evolves; As an alien being—
Alien in whose sensibilities, vision supremely transcend

Synergistically in this divine sculpturing
One becomes alienated from the collective herd;
Yet simultaneously breathes in cadence with God
These few authentic ones of the soil are alienated, isolated;
Yet within them lives fecund Earth
They are authentic inhabitors; Aristocrats of the Spirit
They do not belong with or to the herd's corpses

The traitors to life do belong,
But not to their Selves . . .
Merely to each other—
To that massive blasphemy,
Which in a giant noose, symbiotically intertwines them—
These corpses live off the soil; Not of it—
Trespassing traitors who have aborted the Earth

Terror's slave is a tyrant
   or
A portrait of the perennial Hitler

Born in times of external wars
He revolved into his own bomb
Anxiety pumped his pulse
Calcified his structure, heart, viscera
Dread's footstep walked his shadow

He was but a quiet sound, leaving no tracks
Masking his virulent atoms,
Branded within
The ash of napalm in his marrow

His self a weapon
Aimed to cajole, intimidate, control
Ultimately destroy the spirit-seed
His disguise: The schizoid veils of hypocrisy

He manned his own cannons
His stifled rage, his fuel;
The fallout rabid with
The plague of terror's paralysis

His obsessive propulsions of
Fear and rage
Bred a non-life—
Weighted, possessed
By his own internal bomb
He was poisoned, stained
Within the toxic leaking of himself . . .

In a mansion
He sleeps on a mattress
Framed by the barbed wire
Of his petrified skeleton

Whose dignity has been poison-bitten

    It is not the jungle's genetic creed
     But the humans' blasphemous distortion
    Whose breath curses demands
Upon their children's cradle

        The pristine-eyed deer
           Weathers stormy horns
              The rose smiles fragrant
                  Above fanged thorn

        Why do some green stems
           March on unspiked?
              Or do they mutely shuffle . . .

    Is the deer ever pure
        Whose dignity has been poison-bitten?
            The rose whose face has been aphid-ridden? Or . . .

        Has venom's sword penetrated
      Its stagnant blood
    Coagulating stones
In their veins

        Wrenching them
        From the nurturing milk of innocent's breast

      Casting upon islands of alienation
      Scathed creatures
    Surrounded by the darkening frothy seas
Of an anchoring—knowing . . .

The granite unsupported, falls; boulder-headed

Too many noon-day suns
Whipping flaming heads in orbit
Horns blunted crouch
Mid singed manes ablaze
Viscera seared, Pith culled
Blood winnowed, Wanes

Passion dynamites passages
Tunneling granite's mountains
Exits, Entrances invitation mouthed
Which is Which?

Unfurling light unshadows the eye
Wind deserts the feather's fist

O ended odyssey eternal
You've too many noon-day suns
Too many full-faced moons of
Beams intravenous brooding
Ecstasy's arrow pulses heavy
Impatient to relieve; Transcend

Mercury's blurred body globes
The nightingale's sigh re-echoes

Ended odyssey eternal
The granite unsupported, Falls—
Boulder-headed
Entrances, Exits, Blocked

From life's otherwise flood of domination

For the mind thrashing
Within conflict's grasp
Death thought-duels may offer sport
Ambivalent fencing to indulge

If this sport plays us,
Muscling a shadow mountainous—
Beyond ascent
Its sword crucifies any freedom
Ripping our passport to nascent land

If this sport joins dawn's breath,
Inhabiting one;
The raven's beak pecks . . .
Autonomous decisions are in precision made

If six fingers of courage hold one's sword
This sport may offer transitory freedom,
A releasing—
From life's otherwise flood of domination

Dare Truth's primal drum to beat again

Low in the sky's amethyst dusk
A burgundy blood sun
Glares through the reticence of a darkening forest;
A sovereign spokesman
Somberly raving to his kin,
"Those of singed feather
Brave of brow
You must journey again
Travel my beams up again
Taste me
Allow my bite
Dare my face's fire to consume
Swallow you
Eat your tongues
Blaze in my red breath
Take light into your invulnerable shadow
Free the flames of vision; Your wing-sails
Ascend your breath's wind
Into unbounded flight—
Spheres of another sun; Within

Dare Truth's primal drum to beat again
Re-sulphured in your marrow

Dare to live—live again and again
To fall, fall up again"

The alchemy of transformation is a miracle akin to birth

Staked to her skeletal limbs
Air leaks into fresh openings
Smothered fires now kindled
Roar with cyclonic freedom
Lapping tongues of flame consume . . .

Each hair alight eaten
Blood molten to dark coagulation
Air seared

Her outraged fires blaze
Insistent to swallow her heart's core;
The thickest wood
Of her most noble part

Root, trunk collapse—
Abandoning her worthy tree;
Now a feathery thing
Charcoaled unto ash

A few last embers blink, their last
Freed to wing
Her Phoenix rises

The heavens' blood is sacramental

The heavens teem transparent blood
Into my imbibing pores
I recline on sachet's musk of boggy bergamot
A harvesting of the rain-trees;
Transparent fruits of crystallite-drop

Leaf cheeks fill;
Vessels laden of heavens' nectar
The earth's sustenance swells for root
The stream's glee gushes ceaselessly
Widening curving smiles of bed
Transfused as I in this God's blood

I imbued in reverie, ponder . . .
Of what does water drink, feed?
What if a transfusion were needed?
Only drought rasps response,
"There's a non-substance of her type"

And thought, like a thunderbolt illumined—
As is true of all Deities
All of the infinite seed
She is birthed of herself
Only she is of her blood
She is her own Demeter and Dionysus
And that is why . . .

The heavens' blood is sacred; Irreplaceable
In it, from it, emanates eternity
Of the Gods; is sacramental

I permeated, am transformed
As nature's myriad leaf and tree
In the elysian blood
Of the heavens' benediction

A woo-ing of the soil's constellation's heart

Globes of random bushes ground
Amidst the emerald stalks of spring
Earthly galaxies so root
Fruit bloom in subastral wilds

Jungle stars of pewter leaf
Profiles boned in ivory white
Stem pungently in valiant violet

Upon each pointed finger taut
Myriad gems of rain's formed drop
Bejewel the wildflower's finger royal
A woo-ing of the soil's constellation's heart

The rains shower karats of an opaline gleam
The heavens' vows crystalline bestown
A wedding of miracles in wilderness
Again betrothed in fall

Breathes of the pure innocence of the exquisite

A fawn
in its delicacy
whispers of lace and fern
of the soft chiffon of shadow's dusk
the tremor of petals facing breeze
A fawn
in its hesitancy
murmurs of rustling leaves in eventide's solace
rhythmic in a symphony boundless
The fawn
breathes of the pure innocence of the exquisite

A holiness doth cling

Upon this isle of pagan beach
Passions romp in maverick wilds
Sea-airs heavy of dampened salts

O'er the dunes of solemn sands,
A scattering of dislodged limbs occurs;
Gifts of sculpture, Gifts of truth
Gifts borne of Nature's deaths; Her art
Blanched and polished textures vary
Of the Elements' eternal kiln

Amidst kelp's variegated wreaths
Jewel gentle shells of nacre
Small rock treasures imbued of minerals gleam;
Ornaments divine bestown on
God's cemetery, Strewn
On bones too smooth to wear

At the day's darkest light
Hymns of resonance ethereal chant
Chiming tones of
Lapping tides resound
Overturning beds of rock, Around
A holiness doth cling

Earnest heirs of star-tipped limb

Within the forest's midnight
A glowing twilight lives
Lunar beams enlustre
Nature's tallest heroes
Earnest heirs of star-tipped limb
Stand vespertine enshrouded

Nocturnal shadows pristinely cast
Upon man's black tarred road
Reflect God's sacred art

Dies blushing in her lover's red

The moon sets
Dies blushing in her lover's red
The sun's plumage, within that instant cast
Rouges her unseared cheeks; Envermilion

Irradiant, her surrender cool
Now sinks below indifferent seas
A Renoir silence awes
In an early lavender's dawn

The fortuned eye hugs the bounty
Of this fusion ephemeral
Moments caressed, in time's exquisite timelessness

Behind huddled mountain shoulders
The proud orb master
Of dawn's pale rises
Robed in passion's resplendent flare
His fervent blaze begilds hour's day

Pulses of white heat's loins

Gushing
from the bowl
of its
Blazing womb
The sun's waterfalls stream;
Glistening beams of rain-light's sheen
Flood the voluptuous moss-caped forest
Begilding bough to stem in gossamer's amber
Shimmering seduction's gloss on the leaf's pond-face;
Myriads of glinting mirrors
Reflecting the sun's blood;
Boiling sea inflame
Pulses of white heat's loins
Impassions; Whets the earth
Propagating fruits to harvest's radiance

The drum of pollination beats

A vibrant festival
A gleaming of tribal colors; Florescent

When heaven surrenders herself; All
She gives of her womb
To her dry kin earth
Her essence; Fresh water seas
The rite of rain; A ritual holy

The earth's bowels quake;
The belly laugh of abundant banquet's fare
Waters giggle, in abandon trickle
Gushing down cliffs a-splashing
Vining myriad passages for
Seeds' blood to flow

Fresh waters join the earth's seas' brine—
Hospitable tempest of vast electricities

A waltz, a chant, a chirruping
Budding rhythm's texture—shape
The flavors of the fresh
The spout of mouths a-new

Aquatic laughter rippling,
Resounds air incensed of potpourri

Gypsy wildflowers of butterfly face
Bred extravagantly of
Ancestral pollen—winds
Herald the Eternal's secret
of Life's miracle—seed

continued

Freedom emanating fertility
A mocking of man's cramped vision

The drum of pollination beats;
The ebullience of the wild's pulse
In tribal celebration

The rain feast is lavished
Rejoicing perpetuates;
Bounty germinating of
The heaven's love been shed

I could die with you

You sweeten my mouths
with the milk of you
My mouths so freshly sweet
with our moistures
part, open—fully open
soften to let all of you be
              Within me

O fertile generous milk
that you pour into my body
then drink back from my mouths
              Your milk

This rich milk of you
flows so readily
Its encircling heat—your heat
            Absorbs me

You, my cradle
rock the womb of me
connecting, covering us
with one velvet skin

From your bowels
your walnut voice
moans of our fusion

My being in surrender
melts into your lips

I could die with you

Never have I known a kiss

Upon thought, glimpse, touch of you
The seeds of me, Abandon me
They will fly with any breeze
To settle, grow within you

I feel, see, sense them swell
Swell amongst the heavy nectars
Of the fertile fruits of you

I join you on a verdant vine
Where our succulence can blossom
Our vine leaves touch, then part
Then touch again
In a trembling delicacy

Ripe with sun-basked juice; We kiss
Never have I known a kiss
That ripens me so
As to burst open skin
Offering the tenderest of fruits
Until now, untouched beneath

That unknown design

Gathering the gossamer fleece of abundance
Begot in the warmth of winter's cocoon
Reaped in the quiet of twilight's rest . . .

Fingers now weave to fires
Spinning, spin, spin, the yarns
The multi-colored yarns
The yarns of blood
Of womb and testicle
The yarns that weave
That unknown design
That vast design
As vast as the sky
Or small and tight
And knotted, clotted
Into stillness

And if you can not, all else is less than What Is . . .

When you come to me,
Bring me not, flowers grown of my garden

When you come to me,
Bring me not
The stars off the jasmine vine
But those living in your eyes

When you come to me,
Sperm my eyes with galaxy's light

The star of me rests on the mountain top
I hear the sea's melodic voice below
Its tidal-chant pulses
Refilling my moon-pools . . .
Remoleculed

When you come to me,
Bring your own sea
Your own tides, currents

When you come to me,
Garland my waiting necks
In coils of your humid breath

And to my openings
Ecstasy your pollen
We then be
Infused mutants
Of each other

And tonight the full moon
Reflects platinum undulations
Of the planet-seas

Come to me
With your own full moon
Your own planet

And if you can not
All else
Is less than
        What Is . . .

You were the summer, long before the Summer came

You were the summer, long before the Summer came,
Whilst the rains teemed through light and dark
Resounding the eternal water chimes
Upon my redwood roof—

You were the summer, long before the Summer came,
Entering my redwood home
Of blazing hearth
You brought another fire, Smoldering
Behind your meteorites of eyes

You were the summer, long before the Summer came,
Your solar flames uncoiled
As thirsty serpent tongues—Abound
Lapping my hair, my air
Consuming my winter lakes
The climate changed

You were the summer, long before the Summer came,
Your long beamed fingers flew
Their currents through
Remolding the multi-spheres of me

You were the summer, long before the Summer came,
Soaring to a weightless realm
We are beyond any Time
            Of year

In fevered light

O the fog-filled face of you
Blends with the clouded skies
You drift in the foggy dusk
As another sphere of mist

Through dark glistening eye
Your humid clime envelopes me
As the lowered sky

Only our fevered beams
Burn through this sunless hour
And so light the heavy mist
Of an ended day

You of black moon
Penetrate the dark
With fixed raven eye

Your night imbibes my dusk
We walk home over
Unseen meadows

Our heavy sultry blood
Moves us quickly
In fevered light

owned by Gray

i walk the Gray of night
swimming Gray's air
in Gray's twilight
the seas, skies, sands and me
owned by Gray
this night

In rest without pause

Veiling a silent dusk,
Webs of steamy mist
Swath the pine needle's eye

Woodland lords of russet bark
Fount towers of leaf-sprung crown
Quieter in shade
Smaller without shadows

The fructifying eggplant of earth
Fertilely slumbers, deep in cocoon
Snuggling under her womb-woven shawls of
Musky fruit leaves, nuts, and cone
Deep in cocoon, without
Illuminating rays of heat
To swell open the glance of a seed's lid-eye

Erosion uproots, has dispossessed
The earth's elephant feet of noble trees
Awesome sculptures form
Lightning-charred limbs gnarl;
Lips of dank-mouthed caves
Murmuring mossy vowels of
A sacred ancient code

A veiled silent dusk
In rest without pause

Rhythms of the air's sea

Spells . . .
    of this mossy forest chant
    The air's solitude hums of fertile seed
    Streams of the lullaby breeze, rock leaves
    Cradling ripples in the air

    The wind's rivers flow
    Their spheres unbound
    Freeing forests to rustle's chant
    Orchestration to seed

    Rhythms of the air's sea

But, within me is all of the sea

I wish I weren't afraid of the sea
As he who swims so vigorously
I see the waves as small
Yet they loom gargantuan to fall

I'm panicked by the raging torrents
Knowing them as within me
Riptides, whirlpools may cover my head
Drowning me, unpredictably

I adore watching from ashore
Absorbing the awesome currents
But, within me is all of the sea
And the fear of the sea within me

For those who possess their own theater within

For those who possess their own theater within,
Who reserve the loge seats for themselves,
Having available whatever they care to nibble on . . .

To go to most of society's entertainment
Is an unnecessary distance to travel
And usually less interesting
Than their own dramas within

Our midnight silence fathoms more

In the voice that is locked in my intrepid taciturnity
You, who do not hear my morning words
Now in silence heavy; Apprehend

Behind locked doors
I bathe anointed in jasmine's oils; Yet
The somber redolence of my cavern's disarray
Lurks out; Embalming you

You grit my meanings;
Tangled manes of prowling tigers
Dungeon-caged in conflict

The night of you
Sees beyond the lamp
That unlights your unread newspaper
You guilelessly hum a melody haunting
That I covert with another

Our midnight silence fathoms more
Than our language speaks

A broken tree trunk lies next to you in bed

A glossy full-leafed tree
of medium height
Once stood in the corner
of your bedroom sun

You worshipped this tree
of moistured life

But this tree
began to lean
Its trunk narrow
for its abundant leaves
And its leaves
began to drop

Watching . . .
You began to pour more
then more water
Yet leaves fell and fell
You turned on house heat
A dryness brittled

A passing bird's song could be heard
And the seasons began their change

A broken tree trunk
lies next to you in bed

And you grasp it
Having swept the leaves in your incinerator
a few minutes before

Is it here because the malignancy of the benign is contagious?

Do I write from the fever of virus?
What virus disease is this?
The one bred of what
creeps to stifle?
Closer
      Closer
The ether of nescience encircles . . .

I see beyond their stupor
Into their glaring cavities
As if a fluorescent photo, Was
projected from their chests

I know as their tapes rotate, In
variations of walk and talk
I know behind the clatter
Inside their cavity, Lies
a muscle that dares feign life, With
its hypocritical beat

Their passivity asserts abuse
Daring me, Daring reality

This fever, Is
it here because the
malignancy of the benign is contagious?
Or is it real
Like an animal getting sick?

My spirit wrestles
Dodging the ropy entrails of civilization's nooses

How can there be such violence to blood . . .
God is not in most men.

Weapons of well-known strangers

Cut raw from rusty broken knives
The instruments of strangers
Veins incoherent lie—
Throats gape, betrayed
Gasping dry; Mute
under an alien sun's rage

Amongst the duel's sheathed sword of word,
I recognize such guise
This cloaked deception
Jars my core
My roots are pierced by nails

My fruit-filled vine
Lies bitten-stemmed
Rotting stray to spurring boot

Cut open from the rusty knives
Weapons of well-known strangers

Severed from their source

The churning rage of the sea uproots
Its flowering gardens within
Dispossessed of root
Gardens drift aimlessly
Abandoned to the current's whim . . .
Their mangled bodies beached ashore
Ebb, stagnant to the blanching dry
Scavenged by the sticky fly
Dead offerings to themselves

Severed from their source

Cowards can't resist hate's cheesecloth

Empty people
Bound together by the cheesecloth of rage
This confining cheesecloth controls, strains
Prevents collapse
This perforated fabric
Evenly permits their steady pulse of contempt to drain
Having no hole large enough for another to make contact

Their smiles leer cheese
The theater of hypocrisy
Is filled with volunteers

Without their venom's veneer
The players would be rawly seen
Recognized in their multi-fragments

Cowards can't resist hate's cheesecloth
It cloaks them up big
Others only see the cape's looming shadow
And in fear's darkness, Can't see
Mere cheesecloth casts the shadow

Stagnates in the swamps of Estrangement

Held captive by root—
Origin raped in pollution's sear
Unlike its forest's kin,
The city's tree is gleaned of pungent nectar, scent

Held captive by withered root
Mankind's pith
Stagnates in the swamps of Estrangement

His blasphemous breath
Reeks of choicelessness
In his peristaltic consummation of
Self-generated Drought

At an elegant Swiss Hotel

Like frozen skaters
Waiters glide, pale faces; Stiff
Music played by robot fingers; Dazed
Proper smiles at appropriate times
Revolving doors pushed
By those going around and around

Outside the screech owl
Hoots its feather's truth

The human has killed God, and
Nature stands witness

Entrapped; City Lights

Stagnant boxes
Cement dried into curdled points, Gasp;
Housing for windowless people
Sitting without a blink
Wanting . . .

Door-mouthed
Carpet-tongued
TV'd

The Why of the energy shortage

Within the silence of a bible black night,
Perched high upon the fecund earth of
A wilderness preservation,
I gaze upon the obscene city's glare . . .

Blurred masses of vacant stares
Lidless bulbs unblinking
A wounding blare blisters . . .
Electric eyes; Surrogates switched on
Implants for human vision; Spent

Blindmen reeling
Within their abysmal dark,
For an "On" switch

The dry rot sucks the forest bare and stays as dry

Seasoned timber, orbs dust-filled
Limbs sapped dry, collapse consumed
Leering sticks unmouthed, leaflessly unvowelled
Crucifixes standing; Requiems to their fall
Sockets balded, stare of sterility's alienation
An airless wind webs

At their stubborn clotted root
Skeletons shelled, renounce their earth
The soil's womb seedless shrivels
The wild's grasses dawn aborted
Bark, cone, and limb; Splintered husks;
Multiple burials humiliate selves

Look, see the parasite spineless
So pale green, gauzy;
Beards drape, pose as flimsy, urgent to decay
Smothering loamy bark to desiccated trunk
Clenching in hangman's silent choke
Amputating finger's pine, oak tip
Leeching bough's surrender slow

A grimness lingers unfulfilled
From this plague's indigestible meal

Nature's leper gone astray
Rides the blinded midnight mule
Despair's fungus bearded hovers
Avarice insatiable; Disharmony's appetite
The dry rot sucks the forest bare and stays as dry

Living my mother's Christ
or . . .
Ancestry

I grit the bitter strain
Of the harnessing yoke
Of dragging my mother's ghost womb;
Living my mother's Christ

I leave unploughed
My virgin seed to fruit
Truth's breast to harvest
My burgeoning vine

But, she, they live through my eye
See through my lid
And so much light
Radiates agonies to bear

    Tortoise cheeks pump ether
    Sinking ever deeper to lock, muffle
    Contagious in blood's blindness
    The hollow eye encircles bone

    Heavy lacquered veils of pale
    Relentlessly whisper and claw
    Reeking of virulent dare

    The fume-fogged breath of
    their hollow malignants;
    The anesthesia absorbed
    Before shadow's quicksand devours . . .

    A timeless paralysis strikes
    Without lightning's light again
    The seed-blood ones
    Are bled from their stems
    Eyes, terror-blinded

    Too late for her; Too late
    For so many.

He betrayed himself

When his spirit surrendered
He betrayed himself;
Sacrificing his singular chance
Of growing the tree of his own unique seed . . .
Pawning Life
        for
Breathing Suicide

the predatory One

the predatory One
wings widespread
rigid in no flight
suspended above
watches   observes

is stillness necessary
to capture chosen prey?
is stillness necessary
to see . . .
really see?

when this
jagged jet-feathered One
glides in nearby
he is furtive, suspicious
uneasy on land

why does he
the predator stay
in solitary?

is it a bleak unacceptance
of what he is . . .

A marrowless bone, stone of a person

She was bleached
A marrowless bone, stone of a person
Without a lawn . . .

You married her, and
The forest of you
That grew you tall and mossy
Has lost its seasons
Leaves of green, yellow, crimson
Brittle brown under your feet

The whorling roots of ancestry

You are trapped like so many
Only with you it is more tragic . . .

>   roots that thirst for water
>   bend, choke
>   lean childhood-backwards
>   but the seeds have long agéd dried . . .

Your fresh water springs are spent,
Though once in abundance flowed—
The richest lucent milk
Stagnates now to swamp
Roots starve, shrunken-mouthed
Quicksand greeds

The fresh water springs of you
That once boweled your juicy root
Lustered your raven hair
Blossomed dew in your eyes
Whetted the music of
Your loin-breathed poetry
Carried the gushing rivers of you
To your oceans; Oceans that were you
Now are dry; Dried in burnt dazed eyes:
Two moonless deserts beseeching . . .

Eyes that were the deep green of oceans;
Fathomless oceans tiding promise
Once rooted your
Tall mantic-leafed tree

continued

Now your paths are knotted
You trip on contorted roots
Stumbling mid a circle of selves

The dust of ancestors chokes
Rotting air
Lidding vision

The rocks of you are cleaved
Fissures stare in trance
Bald, without lash's moss

Possession's haunt has sunk
Your howling sun
Sucking it from the skies
It wallows grey; Rays inverted
Midst conflicts mire

The whorling roots of ancestry
Have eaten strong inside you
Appetites great, devour you;
A muscle-eating poison

Tendrils snuff and knot
They tie you up
Your pores smother
There's no more room
        For you

You are pregnant with the dead;
You've immortalized your ancestors
Their lead bones anchor-grip

It is much more tragic for you
You who once rooted
That tall mantic-leafed tree
        In your eyes

A testimony to ageless sprout

Reclining over tumbling waters
Giants have fallen side by side;
Bedfellows nightshirted, emerald-eider-downed
Perpetually in a slumber mossed

Myriad whispery ferns
Flower the leathered bark's moistured pores
Cushioning flanks of dignity's heroes—

Out-flung millennial root
A testimony to ageless sprout

Where once their firmness staunchly stood
High borne heads in stilled peace lie
On earth's pillow's potpourri . . .

O fathomless fountains of birth
You spring eternity's dawn

The sea's night does not seem doomed

The sea's night pulse
Beats of music again
Luna's reflection flickers; Inflames
Illumining surf in Phosphor's blaze
The dark is not opaque tonight

Foam raves in buoyant vigor again
Churning lucent borders to the tide
Not septic with swampy ills;
The lapping spew of inertia

The sea had been convalescent
Its pulse without force of storms
Tonight, its breath has current again
The sea's night does not seem doomed

A lone heathen boulder

A lone heathen boulder
Like an Aztec fortress
Barnacle-eyed
Weathers the sea

Ravaging storm-currented hands
Relentlessly pound, chisel, Sculpting
a hollow out of the stone's silence
Tunnelling a labyrinthian-mouthed cave

Galloping swells of a maverick sea surge sky-bound
Foam-peaked tongues lick glistening air
Fury's churn snorts high in thundering falls
Bolting bodies explode into
A kaleidoscope of prisms
Their wind's water-rhythms chant, Sounding
against and through the mute fortress mouth

Low dewy heavens
Bend beneath the stone arch
Bathing quixotic-tinted moods
Gliding glimmering tides
To the gilded gold
Of the sea's earth of sands

Sunset's lightning streaks
Flood the cave's stone jaws
Illuminating jagged stalactite fang
Blooming the travelling eye
With inflamed deserts of sky

The perpetual force of Nature's quill
Inked by the storm's raging blood
Held constant by moon-reigned fingers
Inscribes strata upon strata
Of her odyssey's log . . .

Her scriptures eternally engraved
As scrolls in the primeval rock

This luminous vessel

Storming seas in the skies tonight
Cloud the moon's crescent vessel
Her beams eclipsed
By the billowing tides
The course of her voyage made hazy

Again and again
The skies' ocean-tides
Seemingly drown
This luminous vessel

But again and again
Her opiate gaze
Floods beyond
The heavens' ocean-waves

As is above is so below

The air's oceans flow
The wind's surf thunders through the trees
Waves sound upon
And through the leaves
Ephemeral music of the air's seas

Transparent oceans of the air
Your storm's rhapsodies may be seen
Sculpturing limbs
Molding spines with your breath

Down below
Within the water's seas
Fish glide the currents of a breeze

Above, birds swim air's waves with flight

Nature contains totality's mobile voice

Ferned fingers of velvet breeze
Caress tilting leaves, stems
Honeyed fingers release seed
Gliding births to outer fields
Permeating air with ambrosial spice of ambered hay
Freeing needle's pungency of pine
Incensing the potpourri of the breeze's dance

Tree's coal-like bark crumbles, peels
Revealing virgin sleekness of sienna skin
Skins released to breathe their wordless essence . . .
Imbue the breeze

Beetles scurry in caverns of rotting wood
Marking change, motion
Juice of blackberries bubbles, sweetened in the heat
Only rock, stone not in time

Twittering, humming, squeaking, buzzing
Every scent, voice, a distinct language flowing
Pollinating the breeze—
Honeyed fingers orchestrating all
In the symphony of fertility's pulse . . .

When the fingers of the breeze
Lie in sleep
The leaves, stems still contain
Totality's mobile voice

Of verdant poets whisper

Within a lake of pregnant air
The eternal seed of
A pubescent woodland breathes . . .

Mooned-white spines
Of verdant poets
Whisper in vowels of transparent tides—
Their ascent to metamorphic gods

The mana of a heavy darkness
Lips all in uterine embrace
The fervid sun's ardor
Wings a lurching brave of spire

The Earth has sprung such fertile child

An untamed stillness speaks

From a patined darkness
An untamed stillness speaks
A slumbering forest breathes
Worlds of fertile scent

Within sublime's depth
Thrives the noble pride
Of trees' rooted truth

Accents Nature's integral kinship

Hidden high in a forest's gully
Madrigals of humming water-voices sound
Their pulsing bells rippling, Chime
tones over octaves of brush and stone
Orchestrating aquatic symphonies, Down
the rocky vertebrae of a steep boulder's fall

The blanched flask of a tree trunk lies nearby
Its hollow silence echoing,
In dignity fallen—
Accents Nature's integral kinship; Ungrasping
A thirst nevermore

When Spirit led man's days and nights

The great surf of a storm-fed day
Breaks distant in the meadow-seas
Pegasus waves of wind-flown mane
Foaming, spray a laughter mad
Rippling banners of their anthem free
Mocking flight of seagull's gray
Purging calmer tides
Claiming somber boulder's brown
Transforming hollows and flatness still
With gushing mouths of waterfalls;
Fountains spouting from some dim rock's crown

The water's foam like some blue-white snow
Churns pure and cold and
Part of the age's time ago, When
The current's universe pulsed,
Harmony intact
When Spirit led man's days and nights